Tales From the Afterlife

Tales From the Afterlife

Fiona Bowie

BOOKS

Winchester, UK
Washington, USA

First published by O-Books, 2011
O-Books is an imprint of John Hunt Publishing Ltd., Laurel House, Station Approach,
Alresford, Hants, SO24 9JH, UK
office1@o-books.net
www.o-books.com

For distributor details and how to order please visit the 'Ordering' section on our website.

Text copyright Fiona Bowie 2010

ISBN: 978 1 84694 427 7

A CIP catalogue record for this book is available from the British Library.

Design: Tom Davies

Printed in the UK by CPI Antony Rowe
Printed in the USA by Offset Paperback Mfrs, Inc

We operate a distinctive and ethical publishing philosophy in all
areas of our business, from our global network of authors to
production and worldwide distribution.

CONTENTS

Dedication

This slim volume is dedicated to the many friends who gently, without a fanfare, led me from a state of indifferent agnosticism to engaged interest in what happens to us when we die.

1. The Sceptic

I closed my eyes waiting for the impact, and the thought flashed through my mind, 'This is it! It's over.' But the sickening thud never came. I found myself surrounded by a whitish gray mist, in which after a moment I could vaguely discern moving shapes. The lorry must have swerved to avoid me, and for some reason I couldn't quite work out at present the summer afternoon sun had disappeared, to be replaced by a thick fog. I tried to orient myself, to concentrate, but felt light-headed, or at least light, as if floating. I shook my head to clear it. I must find the road, avoid a crash. I must have dozed off at the wheel, but at least now I was wide awake. All I needed was to focus, to get back on track. The movements in my peripheral vision started to annoy me. What were they? I couldn't hear cars or voices but knew that I was no longer alone. Someone said my name, in my head. It was as if the sound came from the inside out rather than outside of me. As I reflected on this unusual sensation one of the shapes drew closer and sort of thickened. I felt as if I knew whoever it was, but couldn't quite locate them. A slight sense of panic started to rise up – if I couldn't drive the car in this fog, that would be it, finished. This was hardly the time or place to socialize, I thought irritably. I wasn't getting anywhere. 'Look, what's going on'? I demanded of the rather transparent figure, who was too close, encroaching on my personal space. 'Where am I and what on earth is happening'? The answering voice came into my head again, simultaneously from this familiar stranger and from my mind; 'It's time to go. We are going home.' I was about to protest. I was confused, panicking, but at the same time vaguely curious and rather sleepy. The temptation to just let go and float away with this strange stranger grew stronger. I held on. To give in and allow oneself to fall asleep in a desert or on an ice-field can be fatal. This person was evidently trying to trick me. Whoever she (somehow it felt like a she) was, she would have to be resisted. To keep myself awake I tried to picture my study at home. I had an article to finish. Lunch-time drinks are all very well, but I now needed a clear head, not just to get home. Deadlines won't wait. No copy, no money. As my mind clawed its way back from the dangerous lure of abandonment I suddenly found myself in my study. 'Thank God for that!' was my first reaction. 'How on earth did I get here?' was my second. I must work it out. Something was very wrong. It all looked normal enough, and at least I was home. I must have suffered a temporary memory loss, maybe the shock of the accident, or near miss, had affected my mind. I floated down to my desk and sat down in, or rather hovered a little over, my chair, and stretched forward to turn on the computer. As I reached toward the power button it flickered into life. Weird, but rather impressive, I thought. I reached forward again to turn it off, but before I made contact with the power switch the screen just went dead. It hadn't shut down properly – more wretched temporary files to clog up the memory. But I didn't want to work now anyway. I was tired, so very, very tired. I must sleep. I needed a long, long, deep sleep.

When I awoke I had the sensation of lying in a hospital bed. An extremely peaceful, comfortable one to be sure, and I was aware of people dressed in white uniforms moving around calmly, ministering to patients. Although I felt refreshed my mind refused to reveal the sequence of events that brought me to this place. I remembered with a jolt waking up at the wheel of my car to see the front of the lorry only yards away – to avoid an impact, to avoid being crushed, was impossible. Yet somehow I had survived. I was in hospital. I felt whole, no broken bones, no aches and pains. My memory had evidently been affected, but no doubt this would also recover in time. 'Nurse,' I called. I suddenly felt hungry, and wanted not just food and drink but attention, human company, the reassurance of the familiar. Enough of this nonsense! A thought that had been playing at the back of my mind for some time now began to grow and take hold. I *had* died after all. There was a crash and I did not survive it. But, I reasoned, I wasn't dead. Far from it, I had never felt better. I knew that there was no God, no Heaven, no such thing as the survival of consciousness after death. My existence itself proved as much. After all I could see my body, the bed and bedclothes, the nurses and other patients. No, all would become clear in time. I must just wait a little longer.

Death is the laying aside of the physical body; but it makes no more difference to the ego than does the laying aside of an overcoat to the physical man....

There are some men who cling so desperately to their physical vehicle that they will not relax their hold upon the etheric double, but strive with all their might to retain it. They may be successful in doing so for a considerable time, but only at the cost of great discomfort to themselves. They are shut out from both worlds, and find themselves surrounded by a dense grey mist, through which they see very dimly the things of the physical world, but with all the colour gone from them. It is a terrible struggle for them to maintain their position in this miserable condition, and yet they will not relax their hold upon the etheric double, feeling that that is at least some sort of link with the only world they know. Thus they drift about in a condition of loneliness and misery until from sheer fatigue their hold fails them, and they slip into the comparative happiness of astral life.[1]

For someone who passes into Spirit quickly or traumatically, everything still seems so real to them in earthly terms that they may not realise they have passed over. So they can wander off looking for help, like someone arriving in a new country not knowing where they are. They move from the main railway station or airport seeking directions and get lost.[2]

I woke up finding that instead of never waking up again, I was more alive than ever. The discords within me were so strong that I

4

gave up for a second time, and said, 'you take over, I can't fight any more,' but before doing so I had one last moment of sense to throw out a despairing cry to my mother who passed over some years previously, and she came and salvaged me.[3]

This letter is about a woman who 'died' suddenly as a result of a road accident. Patricia writes:

'You sent me to find Mrs W. I barely know her, but she came over very suddenly and it has been an awful shock. She had never really thought much about it. She couldn't make out where she was, and kept on asking for her dogs and her grandchildren and her husband, and how glad she'd be to see Richard...I was rather nonplussed, but I promised to do what I could and tried to calm her. After a few minutes she yawned and said, Oh my God, I had such a bad night at that hospital I really must go to sleep. Why did they say I was all broken to bits? I'm not. I did feel rotten but that's all over now.' And so I left her sleeping'.[4]

I want to go back to my tycoon whom I left asleep on the sofa. I knew he would wake before his funeral and need help. So I kept a tab on him as Pat calls it and sent out messages to find out his condition. When people began to come into his room I feared he would wake, and so he did. Looking up suddenly he saw me and said, 'Hello, you here again. Who the devil <u>are</u> you?'

'Not the devil,' I assured him. 'Just a guide to explain and help you to deal with this new situation.'

'What situation? Oh yes I know you said I was dead. Well that's a good joke; I'm fine, simply grand, better than I've been for years. I haven't woken up as fresh as this for a long time.'[5]

Then quite suddenly I was tired and they said, 'Sleep here, anywhere, rest for a short or long period.' I found myself lying on the ether, superbly comfortable, warm and contented beyond all description; and so I slept...[6]

2. Laughter

Laugher filled the air like the tinkling of hand-bells. The sound swirled around us, gathering into its train the more sonorous peals from the great brass bells in the tower, mingling with the deeper reverberations of the organ, and all rising, rising in a vortex of luminous, sparkling bands of color, straight through the roof, then leaping high into the sky above. The church steeple spun the threads of sound, projecting them heavenwards – attracting both angels and playful spirits of the air who came to dance among the music's golden strands. Inside the church people were smiling, some chatting. Eyes turned from the polished wooden coffin which sat at the front of the nave to look around. Some may have heard the laughter or caught its vibrations, others merely felt the atmosphere lighten, sorrow and respect turning to wonder and joy. As I looked at each face in turn the many and varied parts of my life resolved themselves into a single narrative. Had I 'kept the faith' and 'run the race'? I had certainly reached the end, only to find that it was instead a new beginning. I laughed again and the air danced and sparkled weaving new colors and harmonies. It had not been an easy life, but even in my darkest moments a dogged steadfastness and sense of humor had somehow pulled me through. I had been ready to go, my spirit gradually loosening the cords that had bound me to my ailing body, until at last I had slipped, like a hand from a glove, into the freedom of the ether. Many old friends came to greet me, and I could have gone with them then, but I wanted to enjoy this last party, to say my goodbyes, held in place by too many ties and unfinished emotions.

The horses had been splendid. I have always loved animals and found the advert in *Horse and Hounds*. 'Just like mum! Trust her to make an entrance' was the children's response, but even the villagers enjoyed the sight, stopping to point and stare at the four black mares with their waving plumes and tassels as they pulled the elegant, if rather poorly sprung, carriage down the lane to my beloved old church. I had planned it all carefully. I left the advert for the horse-drawn hearse with my bank book, where I knew they would look first. In those last months of semi-conscious immobility I found that I could on occasion dwell consciously in the astral world, and gently plant an idea in the mind of my children or friends, or guide them to an object, until at last the whole thing was almost done. When the silver cord that bound me to my body finally gave way for good, I found their minds even more susceptible. They would dream of a hymn and on awakening feel sure that this was the one I wanted. Turning the pages of the hymnal they would find themselves in agreement; 'This was one of her favorites' 'I'm sure she would have chosen that one'. I helped my daughter and niece piece together the pages of my life, with jokes and reminiscences. I didn't want undue solemnity and kindly but hollow sentiments, only real stories and memories of the good times, the fun and ridiculous little incidents that nevertheless become part of our shared history. It was important to me that each one of my family and friends would see the whole of a life, and not just the part each played and the scenes in which they entered or departed. That old photo album and 16mm film were more difficult. I knew where they were of course, but had never told anyone. They weren't really interested, until now that is. I had to plant nostalgia. The children dreamt of childhood places and family holidays at the beach house. It took me the best part of three days and nights to convince my son to open the old wooden box on top of the wardrobe. He didn't know why he should look in there, indeed had never really noticed it was there at all, and it was heavy and awkward to get down. At last I succeeded, and he woke up with a start, staggered out of bed and reached up to grasp the worn handles. The box wasn't locked, which was just as well as I had long since lost the key. That morning, with his sisters, they sat around the kitchen table and talked, talked freely and without the reserve that had built up over the years, while looking at the pictures of our life together. 'It is almost as if mum is with us' said one. 'Well where do you think I am?' I replied, 'In the morgue? That isn't me – just the body that I used. And yes, do make me a cup of tea, it isn't silly at all. It draws me close to you all, and that steaming cup is a powerful symbol of our enduring affection, a love

9

that goes far beyond all the petty squabbles and jealousies that kept us separated from one another.' They seemed to hear, to sigh and feel their hearts warming, clutching the hot mugs with shining eyes that reflected a moment of longing for the time that they too would be drawn home.

Joan is full of laughter. She is the happiest person imaginable; she knows its value on all planes. Laughter sets up a series of bubbles in the ether which reflect light and colour like a waterfall to drop in tinkling cascades of thought into the ether.[7]

Musical thought forms: ...it is easy to calculate that in this case the highest point of the form must rise fully six hundred feet above the tower, though the perpendicular diameter of the form is somewhat less than that, for the organist has evidently finished some minutes ago, and the perfected shape floats high in the air, clearly defined and roughly spherical...Naturally every sound makes its impression upon astral and mental matter – not only those ordered successions of sounds which we call music.[8]

Great power is generated on several planes at these services and you can have no idea how well they can be used....When you are in the etheric body and you attend one of these services, you are the natural link between the congregation (those in the physical body) and Divinity.[9]

Now about healing. So many here have never thought of it. I feel so strongly that we are meant to take our mind and energy into the next body at the end of life, and so make it possible to leave it quietly and easily. As one saintly person said to me, 'I just offered my life back to Christ and he took it.' There are people in all kinds of different states of being, some hardly physical at all, who have so much more of the spirit that I can't see how they can go on living. I met a saintly old priest the other day. He was preparing for another life when I heard him say, 'No, I'll do the new method and slip in and out of a body.'[10]

I was driving down the road – just my normal, everyday drive home from work. All of a sudden, my mother was with me in the car! She was just there with me. I felt her presence, the essence of my mother, as though she was really there. It was almost as though if I had reached out, I could have touched her! I felt a tremendous sense of warmth, a loving warmth and comforting. It was as though my mother wanted me to know she is always there for me. It was a beautiful experience. It lasted just a short while and left me floating, feeling so happy.[11]

3. Recognition

I laughed with surprise. Of course! How could I have forgotten; but I never guessed. Now it all made sense. The painful life just led, but a life rich with opportunities for growth, opportunities to love. That bright, mischievous smile, the many generous gestures – little tokens of affection – the freshly plucked bud, the colorful card, a kiss, "I love you mommy". Now the years of despair and exhaustion began to take on a different hue. When you were happy the sun shone out of you, but to maintain that inner light we had to enter your world. You never really found your place in ours. The childhood battles; getting dressed, brushing teeth, going to school – followed by the searing cry of adolescence – alcohol, drugs, the fall guy who ended up in police custody. The bright-eyed little boy dulled and buffeted by a world that was too harsh for your gentle soul. But through all these years who guided whom? We learnt to love without expectation, without attachment, through anger, disap- pointment, frustration, grief. Grief for what might have been, and for what was. In entering your darkness we found an inner light and strength. Your love for life, and purity of soul sustained and fed our battered spirits. We watched the world's riches fall away as we were brought low by your distress. The dissolution of ambition, increasing poverty, loss of health and happiness. And now – here you are! As the warmth and brightness of the light submerge my being, joy creeps through my weary spirit. My beloved son, my wise old soul, my constant companion, my support in this life and in many others. In your wisdom and generosity you offered yourself as my guide. Through your steadfast inner beauty you protected us from the heavy materialism of life on earth. Your gentle energies helped us to dig deep within, to discover the light beyond the darkness. How much we learnt. Each small act of love, each momentary sacrifice, now shone radiant before me. Each dark moment in which through an effort of will, like one gasping for water in a desert, I cried, 'For You' to some higher power, was now illumined by a luminous cascade of dancing lights. My guide, my 'angel' companion, how little I understood and how much I learnt under your most gracious care.

Most of my subjects report that the first person they see in the spirit world is their personal guide.[12]

Both positive and negative emotions are mixed between soul and host for their mutual benefit. If a soul only knew love and peace, it would gain no insight and never truly appreciate the value of these positive feelings....A soul grows by trying to overcome all negative emotions connected to fear through perseverance in many lifetimes, often returning to the spirit world bruised and hurt.[13]

On the physical plane, where we lack memory of our pre-incarnation choices, we often believe that others inflict experiences upon us. We may respond with fear, anger, hatred, self-hatred, blame, feelings of victimization, or many other emotions that do not reflect our true nature as souls. When we awaken by turning within, we remember that we requested these experiences. We are then free to choose different responses, including gratitude toward those who have made our growth possible. To those we once blamed, we are now able to say thank you. Thank you for caring enough about me to play a role in which you bore the brunt of my anger for many years. Thank you for keeping your promise and honouring our pre-birth contract. Thank you...for allowing me to go through what I had to go through to be the person I am today. Thank you.[14]

This was another 'looking back' letter when Joe saw himself again with Douglas, his only son in his last life, who was killed in France in 1944.

My life in France in the Middle Ages seems to have begun in the north where war and famine and misery and a general chaotic state prevailed. It was all so disorganised that in course of time I seemed to drift south. I remember my meeting with Douglas. I was alone and very thirsty – my men had gone off to their homes to plough the land to try to raise food for their families. I was drifting. Douglas passed me and we looked at each other. I can see him now in the neat simple robe of a clerk, while I was dirty and in rags. Something urged him to invite me into his house for food and wine. I accepted readily and we went together to a small mud *and stone house, very simple, just what an artist would need. 'This is part of the Monastery,' he explained, as he offered me bread and wine. That was the beginning of one of the happiest periods of all my memories...*

Douglas seemed hardly to belong to this world, and I don't know how or when he passed over. But there appeared to be very little difference in our lives...the only thing I noticed was that he had ceased to eat and seemed not to need food or wine...Then I began to notice a certain radiance around him. He was always lightly made or rather spare of form, not heavy like me. One evening I came in from the night when it was quite dark and found him painting with a light issuing entirely from his own body. I can see it so plainly, and my consternation. 'Douglas! What are you doing and where is the light coming from?'

'Me', he said quite simply, 'Don't you understand, I've let go my physical body and am using the next one.'...I do not know how long he was able to continue in this state. It depends on the desire. With Douglas it continued until I was ready to pass on.[15]

4. The Try

As the final whistle blew we erupted in celebration, like so-
many roman candles on Bonfire Night. 'Did you see that
try?' my mind shouted to the crowd of onlookers. An
awkward pass well inside our opponents' half, deftly
caught. Then I ran like the wind, dodging, ducking, until
with a wham my feet were pulled from under me, only yards
from the touch line. The ball flew from my hands and curved
into the air, but like an eel I slipped free, half turned, caught
the ball as it fell, and with a final surge and dive planted it
firmly behind the posts. We had done it, we had won! Now
everyone was leaping around, cheering. Our bodies needed
no rest and our energies were not depleted, but for old-
time's sake we conjured a massive tea with cakes so light and
full of flavor that one slice fully satisfied and sated the
appetite. Some favored orange squash, others tea or beer;
each one summoned refreshment according to his heartfelt
desire.

Getting the team together hadn't been easy. I had

rounded up every Lions cap I could find, old team-mates and our many predecessors. Some took a degree of persuasion, having exhausted their more earthly desires and left for finer realms. Others were fully occupied with other tasks, travelling, teaching, healing of various types, but most of them finally agreed to play, and others to cheer us on. Old age and infirmity were replaced by our most youthful bodies, each in his prime and dressed in something resembling the kit he wore at the height of his powers. We decided to distinguish the two teams not but their strip but by the luminous hue that surrounded their bodies – green for one and blue for the other.

The memories of earthly matches, so slow and clumsy by comparison to our glorious game, had begun to fade but there was one occasion that I still needed to exorcize from my consciousness – to clean and polish and renew, before hanging up my boots for good. I was twelve years old, my first match. I was so proud that my dad had come to watch me. He had been a famous player in his time and I wanted to impress with my whole soul and with every fibre of my being. I dreamt of being 'man of the match'; in sleep I had covered myself and my team with glory, snatched victory from the jaws of defeat. But in that game we call life I was left dejected and defeated. No one passed the ball to me. As I ran up and down the field, longing for some of the action, my fellow players seemed to look straight through me. While my legs grew tired, my spirit dropped like a stone thrown into a deep well. It was as if the game were a bus that never stopped to pick me up. I shouted, 'Over here! I ran and tackled, but the ball had moved on. My youthful inexperience and my shrinking confidence brought me to a stand-still. The new boy no one wanted to know, whom no one trusted. My body may have continued to move but my spirit died, all joy and bravado extinguished. On the journey home I cried quietly, but no one even seemed to notice; it was as if I wasn't even there.

The game in which each one plays their part, each is acknowledged, and no one fails, had worked its magic and restored that piece of my soul-energy to me. The cords that held the old memory in place slipped away as I shone and spun, a kaleidoscope of colors and sound, joyful, light, so full of love and bursting with energy. No longer individuals, we play as a single mind, body and soul. We are a team. We are One.

The painful emotional memories from our past do not die as easily as our bodies.[16]

Oh Ma. I do love this life, you never told me how frightfully well one feels. It's wonderful to be bounding with energy, and able to jump straight off the ground, and stay there! It makes me feel quite heady. I can't understand how our earth could have become so awful, and yet remained within reach of these lovely rays.[17]

There is a statement from the Upanishads of India about our senses being carried in memory after death. I believe this old philosophical text is correct in the assumption that the senses, emotions and human ego are a path to infinite experience, which provides a physical consciousness to the immortal Self. These sentiments were expressed by a client of mine in a cogent way: We can create anything we want in the spirit world to remind us of places and things we enjoyed on Earth. Our physical simulations are almost perfect - to many they are perfect.[18]

After physical death our spirit continues to carry all the fond memories of earthly life. The poignancy of tasting food and drink, touching human bodies, the smell, sights and sounds of walking the deserts, climbing mountains and swimming in the seas of Earth remain with the soul. An eternal mind can reminisce about the motor movements and sensory pleasures of a human vessel and all the feelings it generated. Thus, it is natural souls would want to maintain these planetary memories by re-creating their former bodies in the spirit world. After all, it was here (in the spirit world) where the conceptual design and eventual energy models for physical organisms began.[19]

The ego is steadily withdrawing into himself, and as he withdraws he leaves behind him level after level of this astral matter. So the length of the man's detention in any section of the astral world is precisely in proportion to the amount of its matter which is found in his astral body, and that in turn depends upon the life he has lived, the desires he has indulged, and the class of matter by which so doing he has attracted towards him and built into himself. Finding himself then in the sixth section, still hovering about the places and persons with which he was most closely connected while on earth, the average man, as time passes on, finds the earthly surroundings gradually growing dimmer and becoming of less and less importance to him, and he tends more and more to mould his entourage into agreement with the more persistent of his thoughts.[20]

Dot's home is only partly illusion. She is very near the physical ether which means it is attainable for people without much development who come over with their earth desires unsatisfied, and in the ether of Dot's home, are able to construct just those same satisfying conditions which she had lacked throughout her own earth life...Dot came here to fulfil her earth desires, and they have been long since completely quenched, but she continues to help all those who in like disposition came over with what she calls a 'hot fury' under their skin! Dot is doing a wonderful job, and it is all her own; but having exhausted her egocentric desires, she has called on many of the family and all kinds of more advanced people to help.[21]

There is no time limit to this stage of spiritual life...You choose which friends and relatives you want to meet and they appear to you as you remember them on earth...once the heavy task of clearing your karma is complete and you are a pure spirit of love, you may wish to move forward. Every level or realm in Spirit has a preparation and clearance stage...Every time you are cleansed and purified as you move forward, you leave more of your earthly life behind, losing the attachments that bind you to the physical you once knew.[22]

The Ordinary Person after death...Within...wide limits may vary also the length of their lives upon the astral plane, for while there are those who pass only a few days or hours there, others remain upon this level for many years and even centuries... The average man has by no means freed himself from all lower desires before death, and it takes a long period of more or less fully conscious life on the various subdivisions of the astral plane to allow the forces which he has generated to work themselves out, and thus release the ego.[23]

5. The Disaster

It was a pitiful sight. Some of the children were calling for their mothers and fathers, while parents searched desperately for their children, both among the living and among those who were passing over, unable to distinguish between them, and unaware of what had happened to them. One man dived repeatedly under the water to try to find his infant son. He was so caught up in this task that he didn't seem to wonder or even notice that he could breathe underwater, or that he could pass through the side of the sinking ship with ease. People clung to one another, most in a state of shock, as they rose up out of their bodies. A few more advanced souls among them quickly realized the situation and started to help us.

When something like this happens there are many from our side who are on hand to help. Some have their own special task or skill, and are happy to teach relative newcomers like myself. I learnt how to build rescue stations for the many souls who come over in a state of complete disorientation. Others were engaged in the delicate task of gathering up the etheric bodies and gently disentangling them from the physical. There are gentle souls who have a special gift for talking to those who are crossing over, finding the right words and phrases to put each one at ease. If, as in this case, everything is in a state of confusion, with the living, dead and dying all mixed up together, it can be quite hard to persuade some souls to trust us and to leave the scene. We explained that we were part of the rescue party and that they should come with us to a place of safety. We promised them that we would look for their friends and relatives, and to reunite all those who had crossed over at the same time. We then took them into the higher ether, away from the immediate scene of the disaster. As many of those who drowned were used to a hot climate and desert conditions, we created an oasis with comfortable tents, not too luxurious as it was important that they had time to adjust gradually to their new situation, and we wanted them to believe that this was indeed a relief camp rather than a strange exotic dream from which they would presently awake. There were camp beds where they could rest, and soothing music. We gave them water and sweet tea, which not only calmed them but which also began to restore their energies. The next task was to persuade them to sleep.

There was one woman who insisted on going back to look for her mother. As she would not be dissuaded I accompanied her. We found her mother, quite uninjured, but very cold and wet, clinging to a small liferaft. We could see the rescue vessels, and as dawn was already breaking she had every chance of being found alive. It was tricky to persuade the daughter to come away with me again. She clung to her mother and cried, and kept repeating that she was safe, and that they were going to be all right. Although the young woman sensed that something was amiss, as her mother was not responding, she hadn't yet understood that she had crossed over and that her mother could neither see nor hear her. Then she saw her body floating face down in the water near the life raft, and became even more agitated and confused. I do believe, however, that the older woman sensed her daughter's presence. She seemed to relax a little, almost to smile. A little color returned to her pallid face, a flicker of hope, and then a blush of pink in her cheeks reflected the first rays of sunlight, reaching out across the water towards the raft. You could see that she now dared to believe that she would survive, and that the rescuers would find her. I don't think she saw the lifeless body in the water, so in that moment, with her daughter beside her, knew in her heart that her daughter was indeed alive.

I had to be quite firm, telling my charge that it was time to go, that she could visit her mother again, but that as she had had such a shock she must first rest. I think she began to understand that she had survived the death of her body, but didn't at all know what to expect, and so was quite lost and afraid. When we returned to the camp a nurse gave her some golden-colored nectar to drink which sent her quickly into a deep and peaceful sleep. Her guide was nearby, on-hand for when she woke up, so I felt happy to leave her then, and to get back to the task of reuniting loved ones with one another, and with comforting those who had come over alone.

The Isle of Man Disaster: I was in Douglas when this awful thing happened, and it was terrific, and if seen from your side only it was horrific. But there was another side... Children can be so amazed by being shown a vision that they are quite impervious to physical pain. They allow their consciousness to flow into the exciting beauty which is flung within scope of their vision, and while this moment lasts the bodies are separated, and Flo took them all far away from the scene in the twinkling of an eye.[24]

At what is called death, the etheric double is drawn away from its dense counterpart by the escaping consciousness; the magnetic tie existing between them during earth-life is snapped asunder, and for some hours the consciousness remains enveloped in its etheric garb.[25]

I want to tell you about the ship that sank. I wasn't there but I've been there since it happened. I don't know how quickly those men trapped in the ship were able to leave their bodies, but I gather it was fairly rapid and quite unexpected. Having got free, of course, they were able to lift themselves on to the surface and were soon helping to raise the submerged ship. It was the most extraordinary scene. When Pat took me there I found a number of ships round the sunken one, with men climbing about in and out of the water. At first I couldn't distinguish those in the body and those out of the body. To me they looked the same until Pat explained that those in our sort of bodies were plunging down without diving suits and coming up shouting to the rest, giving directions which no-one seemed to understand, going up to their old mates and bellowing in their ears, but there was no response. I saw the look of utter amazement in the face of one obviously able seaman when no orders he'd given were carried out.

'What can we do'? I asked Pat.

'Call a halt and ask them to come aft for a drink.'

We did so – they were thirsty – but couldn't see her.

Next time I looked at Pat she'd taken on the look and uniform of a seaman. 'I'm making them see me now,' she said. 'If we can get them to relax and drink hot coffee we'll get them to sleep, and then they can be taken away from all this, and cease to feel frustrated.'[26]

You asked me to comment on the old palace at Knossos; but I couldn't find anything there. It was all much too old – full of memories, but even the wraiths had left; and anyway I was much more interested in the battlefields...

I soon came upon some army huts in the etheric, and on stepping inside in my usual brusque way, I found a sergeant in charge of the orderly room. He looked up and welcomed me in a semi-army way. I don't think he saluted, but he got up, and called me 'Sir'. I asked what he was doing, 'Running the camp, Sir, and keeping the Mess going for the duration.' I said, 'But the war ended 18 years ago. What do you mean by the duration?' He laughed and said 'Not that duration, Sir. We are rather 'out-back', but not so far! We are keeping this place going for the chaps who can't get settled into the new life. They come over so quickly. Some have gone home – no-one recognised them. They'd never thought about a future life and they just didn't know what on earth to do with it. So we decided to build a camp on army lines, and let them all make a base here until they found their feet. Many of them enjoyed it all so much we can't get them to move on; but there's no hurry...Then as the other battlefields set up similar bases, some chaps came and visited us and we got them circulating. I was just one of them myself. I didn't come over like you, Sir, knowing a lot. I came over very green, and was I frightened when I found myself out of my body, drifting about? I hung on to earth, it was all I knew, I wasn't going to lose touch if I could help it. Hundreds of others felt the same. We were like drowning men searching for anything we could hold on to that was familiar. We have wonderful Spirits here at times. They come and teach us how to move, and think, and use our new powers. It's all very interesting. I'm quite happy to stay on for a bit longer, but I'm beginning to feel a desire to go on, but I've signed on to stay here until the camp closes'.[27]

Spirit helpers are always nearby to collect and escort new arrivals to the reception areas in Spirit where they can adjust to their new lives.[28]

6. One Last Drink

We pass the time congenially enough – a game of cards, then tiddlywinks. A slow pint that lasts all evening; we argue and discuss the merits of horses versus tractors, the price of pigs and whether it will rain at Michaelmas. Old George doesn't really say much, just grunts and sucks on his pipe. He doesn't like the noise or the comings and goings, especially when a group are sitting in our alcove, sometimes almost on top of us. People are so loud and so rude these days, hardly even make the effort to say 'Hello', not that it bothers us. We have our own company and like it that way. When he gets really annoyed, like when those lads and lasses were larking around and showing no respect, George sometimes bangs his tankard on the table – just to get some peace and quiet. There was even a time when he threw a beer mat at a young lad who wouldn't stop shouting. The boy had evidently had a few too many and didn't know when to stop, or couldn't hold his bitter. That shut him up pretty quick. Everyone in the room stopped talking and the group sitting in our alcove were out of there before you could say 'Jack Robinson'. We had a good laugh at that one. Even George was chuckling, not exactly smiling, but you could see that he was pleased with himself. After that people sort of avoided our corner, and we could mind our own business without anyone bothering us. Things have changed around here though. Many of the old farmers have stopped coming. They used to come in on market day when they had a bit of money from selling off their lambs, or when they had a cow or horse surplus to requirements. Perhaps it is the price of beer these days – we can hear people grumbling about it although ours is always on the house – they never ask us old regulars for money.

One young lady – and you get far more of those coming in these days, sometimes whole groups of them, not a lad among them, and the wives who should be at home making the tea – anyway, this one complained to the lad behind the bar that someone was smoking in our corner. Well of course we were! Jack has his pipe, and George and I like to roll a cigarette. The bar man didn't believe her at first, but she insisted he come over and sniff around. And as Jack puffed away, Alf came along to join us, and he lit up one of those small cigars, so there was quite a cloud of smoke. I used to have a bad chest but it has cleared up now, and the smoke doesn't bother me at all. Anyway, this barman agrees that he can smell it, and we can see other people coming over to have a sniff. Quite comical really, but why a bit of smoke in a pub should cause such a fuss I can't imagine – we have always smoked as we drink our beer, and enjoy one another's company. Well, the next thing you know a plaque goes up on the beam over the alcove, the one with all the horse brass and the stuffed carp that old Will pulled from the meer the summer of the drought, the year the water almost dried up leaving the fish stranded in a few inches of muddy water. This plaque, well, it said the pub was haunted. Haunted, I ask you! We have been here for years and haven't seen any ghosts. If anyone knew about the pub being haunted it would be us. They could have asked us but people these days, they have no time for the old folk.

The problem with that plaque is that instead of leaving the place alone, more people started coming, and even making a point of sitting in our alcove. There was some story about the Hanging Judge, you know the one, Judge Jeffries they called him. Held assizes up and down these parts and, like many of the old inns, the room upstairs was used as a court house and the courtyard as a place of execution. They are saying that both the Judge and some of his victims are still around here; don't know they are dead, and can be seen re-enacting their last hours. I think they must be soft in the head myself. Old buildings have an atmosphere and creak a bit, it makes people uneasy and they start imagining things. Then some young men arrived with all sorts of contraptions, calling themselves ghost-hunters, and set out to measure the temperature, and goodness knows what else. I have to confess we decided to have a bit of fun with them. Well, not much happens these days, one day is much like another, so it was a change, something to do. They kept asking whether there was anyone here, and if there was a spirit present would he show himself? We felt a bit sorry for them, not having seen any ghostly judges or cattle thieves or such like, so eventually Jack starts tapping his pipe on the table, and these ghost-hunters are so excited that George leaps up and heaves the carp off the wall. He didn't mean to damage it but it must have been heavier than he expected because the case slipped out of his hands, narrowly missing Alf's head, and smashes on the floor. I don't know what they used to preserve it but there was quite a stink. The ghost-hunters were trying to stay calm but you could see they were rattled, and the smell was evidently too much for them as they packed up pretty quick, leaving the mess for the landlady to sort out in the morning. We were sorry about the old fish, but it didn't do the pub's business any harm. There have been more people than ever since then, whole coach loads of them. Perhaps that is why they started this ghost rumor in the first place, although why they should think the Judge or some wretched laborer should be interested in throwing a fish around I can't imagine! All in all the effect has not been good – it just isn't the old Black Lion that we used to know and we are pretty fed up what with all the comings and goings and everything. Even the beer is losing its taste – they must have switched breweries. Anyway, we are all agreed that we are going to move on soon, just as soon as we can work out where to go next. That's the thing, where to go next.

It is a sad, but true fact that people who have not fully passed on into the spiritual realms... find themselves in what we term 'No-Man's-Land', an area between the earth plane and the 'first' spiritual realm. It is not the place of fire and brimstone threatened by zealous preachers...However, for one reason or another, some people become trapped in their own earthly space and time...

People in this area are still almost physical in vibration, and can produce physical phenomenon [sic] including poltergeist or ghostly activity.[29]

The popular religious teaching of the West as to man's post-mortem adventures has long been so wildly inaccurate that even intelligent people are often terribly puzzled when they recover consciousness in the astral world after death. The condition in which the new arrival finds himself differs so radically from what he has been led to expect that it is no uncommon case for him to refuse at first to believe that he has passed through the portals of death at all; indeed, of so little practical value is our much-vaunted belief in the immortality of the soul that most people consider the very fact that they are still conscious an absolute proof that they have not died.[30]

This letter is from my daughter Patricia, who came in spirit to the Memorial Service of a Master of Fox Hounds who had not given much thought to 'what happened next'. He passed over suddenly with a heart attack:

You called on me yesterday to meet B.S. I was proud to be asked to meet that splendid looking person...I was delighted to be able to go up to him and say, 'I'm the eldest of the Sandys daughters, they've sent me to welcome you.' He just stared at me as though I was quite crackers, and then he said very slowly, 'One of the Sandys girls from Himbleton? I remember you and your sister — but what on earth are you doing here?'

'Well, I'm not exactly on earth, that's the point.' I answered. But that didn't click.

He was watching the ceremony and the service. Suddenly he

33

caught his name being mentioned. 'Just as though I wasn't here myself – never got any notice to attend this service,' I heard him mutter, 'Always went when they asked me; everyone looks very depressed. What's it all about?'

I was standing quite close to him, and whispered; 'I think you'll understand soon.'

'But, God bless my soul, why shouldn't I understand now? And why are we standing in the aisle? You'd better go and find your family, and I'll press in here.'

He did so, finding to his surprise that no one made way, or took any notice of him. He looked so worried that I came closer and whispered, 'Don't you see, it's your *Service, all planned for you...You knew it wouldn't be very long before you came over to us, and now it's happened, and they are all wishing you God Speed.'*

He accepted it quite simply, and in the most practical voice he turned to me and said, 'Am I dead...? It seems an odd thing to ask a girl, but you seem to know what it's all about.' So I agreed and urged him to go with me right up to the altar, and stand quite close to the Bishop. When the Blessing was given, such a draft of spirit power was invoked that we escaped straight through the roof on to another plane of living.'[31]

7. Falling Back

Oh I had had my opportunities all right, but I had not taken advantage of them. The funny thing is, I was so confident. I really believed that I had done well, passed all the exams, ticked all the boxes. I had been faithful, some even said fanatical. I had prayed, although to what I am not sure now. The God that I had created resembled a crazed dictator at times, a product of my fear of failure and my inadequacy. I did as the Scriptures dictated, insofar as I or anyone else could decipher them. I gave alms to the poor, whether it was to the sad-looking woman selling magazines on the High Street, responding to disaster relief appeals on the TV, or packing boxes of toys and sweets for refugee children. How superior and generous I felt, so different, so far above the recipients of my charity in circumstance and wealth. If I had at least learnt to see them as brothers and sisters, or could have put myself in their shoes, I might have been a little more generous, or even have stopped to talk to the men and women sitting on the pavement with their grubby sleeping bags and skinny dogs. If instead of secretly blaming them for their predicament, or feeling sorry for them, I could have got to know them, and shown some fellow human warmth, I might have taken an interest in their lives, in their hopes for the future and their dreams. It might have been different. I might have been different. Instead of liberating me, reading the Scriptures and communal worship seem to have simply helped build a wall around my fragile sense of self. On one side were like-minded 'good' people, comfortable, complaisant, innately conservative. On the other, well on the other side were the rest – everyone. Those I feared, those I was indifferent to, and even the few I loathed (or thought I did, it is strange how differently we see things on this side).

I didn't do anything so terribly wrong. It was an acceptable, even a good life in the eyes of the world. I was faithful to my marriage vows, respectful to my parents, caring for them in their old age, at some personal and financial cost to myself and to the grandchildren. I made a real effort to get on with my neighbors, I didn't drink or smoke, and avoided most common vices, even when tempted. I looked after my body. I ate healthily, walked to work, and after retirement still worked out once a week in the gym, or made an effort to go to the swimming pool. I never 'let myself go'. But now, played out before me are the opportunities missed. My original intention was to have a life of relative ease and security in order to focus on the little things, but I fell prey to selfishness and my goal was distorted by my pride and so-called faith. It was a life of surface and appearance, but with little depth, and I now see how little real joy.

From earliest childhood to my final breath there were so many chances to love, so many opportunities to light the divine flame in my soul, and my guides certainly worked hard to remind me, to provide the opportunities, but they found it hard to attract my attention. I was so busy 'being good' and justifying my existence that I felt little need for advice or help from others.

Only a very few incidents among the years stand out, and shine a little more brightly amid the dull browns and reds of my earth-bound selfishness. There was the occasion on my twenty-first birthday when I saw an injured dog on the road. I had my new car, and was so proud of its shiny mock-leather cream upholstery. I drove past, but found myself unable to continue and went back to help the dog. It was too badly injured to object when I picked it up and put it on the back seat – my lovely new car was full of hair, blood and mud. I never quite got rid of the smell of urine and frightened animal. I took the dog to the vet, paid the bills, then fetched him home and nursed him. I put up with the mess, the dog hair in the carpet and on the sofa, and treated him kindly over the years. I never even liked dogs, although with time a certain affection grew between us. Then he died, many years ago now, although 'died' of course is just another way of saying that he moved on, moved right in, and now here he is, jumping, licking my hand, barking, wagging his tail as if that first act of kindness towards him were enough in itself to win me a place in heaven.

And then in the middle of the over-harsh and cold growing years of my children (for that is how they seem to me now) there was a time when I stopped to listen, to really listen. Relationships had been strained and her behavior on that occasion was way out of order, far beyond what we could accept. Instead of demanding an account I silenced the inner judge for a moment and tried to enter her world. What had upset her so much? I took her pain on myself, not belittling the lovers' tiffs and imagined slights, but soothing her teenage tantrums and traumas with my love, infusing a sense of security and wholeness into her fragile spirit. OK, I had help, although I didn't know it at the time. That urgent call wrung from my soul, calling upon some higher power to give me the wisdom and patience I sorely needed in that moment had been heeded. The comfort that I gave, and the warmth and trust that, for a while at least, returned to our battered relationship, was the fruit of that cry for help. A channel opened up between 'heaven and earth'. My guides and my higher self were able to pour down concentrated love and peace, surrounding us in a golden glow of protection and healing.

Another light shone, as if on a stage or diorama and I looked with amazement at an incident so slight and insignificant that I had almost no memory of it at all. I certainly hadn't weighed it in my bank of credit. I was in an airport lounge, waiting for a flight. A cleaner, foreign and evidently tired and heavily pregnant, was moving among the cafe tables, sweeping up the discarded cups and paper napkins, the plastic spoons and crumpled newspapers. A half-eaten croissant lay under the table, and the chairs and cases blocked her access to it. I glanced at the hopeless, defeated expression, and without thinking bent down and picked up the offending pastry, and tossed it into the open black bin-liner fixed to the end of her mopping trolley. As I straightened up our eyes met for a moment and a smile of gratitude flashed across her face. I nodded, and in that brief encounter there was an acknowledgment of our common humanity. I wiped my hands, picked up my suitcase and left to catch my flight, thinking no more about the incident until I relived it in this place of inescapable clarity. These are small crumbs indeed to take with me from an earth-life, I can see that now, but each one is nevertheless weighed and given its true value. I will have another chance to learn those lessons, perhaps in a situation that gives my selfish ego less opportunity to pull me down. After all, the only goal of our life on earth, as my guides gently remind me, is to become perfect in love.

It is well for us to bear in mind that there is a hidden side to life – that each act and word and thought has its consequence in the unseen world which is always so near to us, and that usually these unseen results are of infinitely greater importance than those which are visible to all on the physical plane.[32]

Souls who come before their respective councils have been debriefed during orientation sessions with their guides. However, it is in front of the council where souls feel most vulnerable about their past performance...The purpose of the Elders is to question the soul in order to help them achieve their goals in the next lifetime...Actually, souls themselves are their own severest critics.

So that they can properly plan for our future, the Elders want to make sure that we totally understand the consequences of our actions, particularly toward others.

The Elders ask us how we feel about major episodes in our life and our courses of action. Desirable actions and those that were counter-productive are discussed openly with us without acrimony or finger pointing. Regardless of the number of times we continue to make the same mistakes, our council has enormous patience with us. We have much less patience with ourselves...

The council is looking to see if the inner immortal character of our soul maintained its integrity in terms of values, ideals and action during incarnation. They want to know if we were submerged by our host body, or did we shine through?...The council is not so concerned about how many times we fell down in our progress through life, but whether we had the courage to pick ourselves up and finish strong.[33]

I have often been a man; my feminine lives were considerably fewer and not at all happy...I can feel my French womanly self more easily but I was cold and remorseless even then. It was really only in my last life that I attained understanding of the human being...I have to become that which I then was and relate that wisdom only to the highest motives. Over and over again I failed but the Christ puts us on our feet, and we reluctantly try once more.[34]

Often when people speak of giving and receiving, they are referring to gifts of action, or material things, but the Law of Attraction *is not responding to your words or actions, but instead to the vibration that is at the basis of those words and actions. Let us say that you see those who are in need of something. Perhaps they have no money, transportation or food. And as you see them, you feel sad (because you are focused on their lack and activating that within your own vibration), and from your place of sadness you offer them the action of money or food. The vibration that you are transmitting is actually saying to them, 'I do this for you because I see that you cannot do this for yourself.' Your vibration is actually focused upon their* lack *of Well-Being and therefore, even though you have offered money or food through your action,* your dominant offering is perpetuating their lack. *It is our encouragement that you take the time to imagine those people in a better situation. Practice the thought of their success and happiness in your own mind, and once that is the dominant vibration that you hold about them, then offer whatever inspired action you now feel. In that case, because of the dominant vibration of your Being, as you are holding them as your object of attention, you will attract a matching vibration of Well-Being from them. In other words, you will uplift them. You will assist them in finding the vibration that matches their desire for Well-Being instead of the vibration that matches their current situation. In our view, that is the only kind of* giving *that has value.*[35]

There are those who do things 'for love'. There are those who do things trying 'to be Love'. Those who do things 'for love' may do them well, but, thinking they are doing a great service for their neighbour, who is sick for instance, they may annoy with their chatter, their advice and with their help. Such charity is burdensome and inappropriate. They may gain merit, but the other is left with a burden. This is why it is necessary to 'be Love.' Our destiny is like that of the planets; if they revolve, they are; if they do not, they are not. We are, in the sense that the life of God, not our life, lives in us, if we do not stop loving for one moment. Love places us in God and God is Love. But Love, which is God, is light and with the light we see whether our way of approaching and serving our brother or sister is according to the heart of God, as our brother or sister would wish it to be, as they would dream of it being, if they had beside them not us, but Jesus.[36]

Sally, Nov.26th 1984: Aunt Helen? Yes she is awake, and very glad to have finished her earth life. Dogs and horses clatter round her as personal friends and individuals. It's a most amusing sight. She was met by all her old ones, and every animal she had ever loved streamed up demanding to be remembered. I love being with her, and I am learning more about their ways of thought and feeling. The horses are so intelligent, I can feel that now, as she does, that they are not just one move away from us, but that some are definitely on a higher plane. The dogs are often very much the same. They have opened to me a whole series of vibrational planes, and shown me unexplored gifts and abilities. The animal world is here to teach us our lack of power to use the vibrations around us. Dogs and cats show us how to draw life and healing out of a flower, a tree, or even a nettle! What do you think of that?[37]

This next stage of life, what could be called 'level three' is for training, but it is also where babies, very young children and pets are received and live. Apart from losing a parent or loving partner, the loss of a child or a beloved pet can bring the greatest heartfelt sorrow. Bereaved parents and animal lovers should know that after clearance children, and pet animals and birds that have had a close and loving bond with a human, arrive directly here on this beautiful level.[38]

8. Play Time

I wasn't afraid to die. I knew that I would. When my sister died first I was jealous, but we are twins, identical twins. We shared everything, including the illness, and so I knew it would be my turn soon. We used to play together in our angel world, in our dreams. But sometimes when we were awake we would go to our secret place and sort of day-dream, and have such adventures and play with our friends. It could be raining outside but in our summerland it never rains. There are trees to climb and flowers, a lake and a river for swimming, and forests and meadows. We can eat as much as we like, whenever we want to. It doesn't matter if it is meal-times or anything, we just think about ice-cream or chocolate cake, or orange juice, and there it is. There are some grown-ups who sort of look after us and try to give us lessons, but not in a bossy way and mostly we just run away and play. No one follows us and we never get into trouble for it. So when my sister left her body behind I knew that was where she had gone.

43

People looked at me strangely at the funeral as I never cried at all. Apparently I had a big smile on my face, but that's because she was jumping around, pulling faces and making me laugh, only no one else could see her. They didn't understand and thought I had gone soft in the head or was being naughty. Then I got very sad because I was on my own and could only see her in my dreams. Day-dreaming my way to summerland was much harder on my own and I got so afraid that I might forget about summerland, and about our other friends. I could never forget what she looked like or the sound of her voice because I only had to look in the mirror or to say something. We are that alike – best friends too. We have been together for ever so many lives, but not as twins before. We thought it would make a change, be fun, but it was a bad life and we decided very quickly that we would leave it and try again with different parents.

Our earth life was never as good as summerland. We were often afraid of the shouting and the cold and hunger. They weren't exactly cruel but they didn't know how to look after children, or maybe they just didn't really try very hard. So sometimes they would forget to feed us, or go out and leave us on our own and we didn't know when they were coming back, or who would come back. And that could be worse than being left on our own. That's why we used to spend so much time hiding in our secret place, where we could escape back to our other, real home. After a bit, on my own, I just wanted to join her. There was nothing left for me on earth. Everything seemed dark and cold and empty and I didn't understand why I had to wait, why we couldn't have gone together. When my turn came I was excited and only a little bit scared. It felt like ages, but it was less than one birthday, and now we are together again. Towards the end, when I was ill in bed, I found that I could leave my body more easily and she was always there, waiting for me. She looked a bit older, but so healthy and full of life and fun. There is no sickness or hunger in summerland and grown-ups are always kind to us, and show us how to do things. We are leaning how trees grow and how insects are made, and how to help them with our energy. But mostly we just play.

A primary, or principal soulmate is frequently in our life as a closely bonded partner. This partnership may be our spouse, brother or sister, a best friend, or occasionally a parent. No other soul is more important to us than a primary soulmate and when my subjects describe lives with these souls as their mates most will say their existence is enriched beyond measure. One of the greatest motivations for souls to incarnate is the opportunity for expression in physical form. This is certainly an attraction for primary soulmates.[39]

Patricia: Ma, I am told that children all wake up in a lovely place of their own imagining. Each child has a place of retreat locked in his own mind. It may be a picture which recalls something of his (or her) pre-natal life. In any case all children when asleep go to that sweet garden of their own minds, and they wake up on earth either refreshed by the contact, or depressed when the earth vibrations touch them and they find the contrast too great. One little boy came over with a picture of the Zoo in his mind, and so on waking he found himself back in the Zoo; but all the animals were free and friendly, and he was invited to feed them from familiar things like paper bags, and he immediately became so excited that his vision grew fast and he began to see all the other children. Some were in dream bodies, and others like himself had come over altogether.[40]

Edie: I love meeting children because they have generally come over owing to their having no further need of the physical body and are unconsciously developed souls. I have a child with me now in this room, she has been very unhappy and unloved and so I bring her into a love atmosphere of gaiety and happiness, and watch for the return of colour to her aura.[41]

In sleep, the astral body, enveloping the consciousness, slips out of the physical vehicle, leaving the dense and etheric bodies to slumber.[42]

Twins are friends and equals, having shared their mother's womb for nine months, or often, according to the Bangwa, much longer. Before birth they roam the world of spirit children for indefinite periods before conception...

Twins are wonderful children, likened to 'spirit beings' and called 'children of the gods'. They are thought to be endowed with the gift of seeing their way back to the world of unborn children (efeng)...Children have to be seduced from efeng into their mother's womb. In some cases they go in pairs and are born (in the ideal case) as twins.

Other children, who exhibit signs of chronic illness, are said to suffer from the tormentings of their 'friends' in efeng who have not agreed to be born and who continue to seduce their friends along the road to efeng and the carefree life of the unborn children.[43]

46

I had become a mass murderer by the time I left my second family, killing off in my head all the children who had come and gone, sharing my room for a month or two. I didn't even know you were meant to mourn. Instead I just wished I was dead too and roaming again in the heavens with my other Spirit friends. But it's too late. I've got what I wished for – a successful rebirth...

We play every day after teatime by the sandpit. I teach Annabel how to fly out of her body and make friends with the Angels. I ask the Angels not to let her die, now that she knows who they are. I pray to God not to let Annabel go to heaven. But the Angels don't listen to me, and God forgets to answer my prayers...

When I arrive outside a big white house, surrounded by a tall fence of barbed wire, Annabel surprises me with a visit. She hovers above my head and makes my face feel warm. She whispers: 'I told you so.' I ignore her and look down at my feet and see a caterpillar crawling along the ground. I know it's Annabel trying to reach out to me, I can hear her whispering: 'Friends forever' just like the days we used to sit and play beside the sandpit in the Village. I stamp on it and my ears are screeching with Snake's call. Annabel turns into a yellow butterfly and brushes my forehead goodbye. I try to catch her, but she's off up in the skies.[44]

The children's playground in Spirit is where all the children who pass over at an early age live, share and play and are brought up in the Light. Unlike in parts of your world, no child is neglected or forgotten for they are looked after by spiritual people who love children. There is great joy here, and it is uplifting to pass through this level and see so much beauty that there is in a child. There is a Children's Academy where little ones are also taught that their parents are also individual spirits following their own pathway, and when they are all eventually reunited, they do not have the same dependency of child to parent as in the physical.[45]

9. Earthbound

My first thought was that I had failed again. I had tried so hard to make sure this time, even said my goodbyes. I parked the car down the bottom of the farm track where I knew that I would not be found, at least until daylight. I didn't want anyone to stop me, no good Samaritans or misguided philanthropists. I didn't hesitate or look back. I had had enough and craved the relief that would finally come with the enveloping cloud of total oblivion. The sweet finality of death. As the car filled with fumes I gagged and felt light-headed and nauseous. I forced myself to take deep, even breaths – I couldn't afford to screw it up this time. In the gap between the clouds the moon suddenly picked out a badger following its customary trail from the woods to the stream, but the startled animal suddenly stopped and sniffed the air. The sound and smell of the engine or sight of the car across its path brought it up short, and it turned suddenly and headed back up the hill. My head swam and I began to drift into semi-consciousness. I was roused for a moment by a screech just outside the car, and dimly registered an owl in front of the windscreen. 'This is it,' I thought, and was overwhelmed by a sense of relief and gratitude that it was finally all over. The gnawing despair and lethargy, the sense of never belonging anywhere, the disappointments I had suffered – all this was behind me now.

It was not just me who had suffered, but those I had let down time and time again. They would now be free of me and at last I would find release. But instead of the finality of extinction, I was floating around in a gray mist, still very much alive, but disconnected. I was vaguely aware of other people but couldn't see them. I assumed that somehow the car had run out of petrol and the engine cut out before its work was done. I was so angry at having messed up again – how many more times could I find the resources in myself to plan and stage my own death? Yet the alternative, to carry on in a living hell, was too awful to contemplate.

As dawn broke I became aware of the car just below me. I seemed to be viewing it from the outside, as if I was somewhere just above the bonnet. The engine was still ticking over and fumes were leaking out from the gap at the top of the window where I had tried to wedge a piece of flexi-drainpipe. The other end was pushed over the car's exhaust, held in place with black plumbers' tape. I could even smell the stinking cloud of petrol that now enveloped the inside of the car, and formed a heavy white cloud around it – although for some reason the fumes no longer seemed to make me feel nauseous or affect my head. And then I saw it, which gave me a shock, as if a charge of electricity had suddenly been shot through me. I saw a body slumped over the steering wheel of my car. In a moment of panic I thought someone else must have been in the car with me, and have died in my place. I had never intended to hurt anyone else, and now what had I done? Then with an even greater sense of shock and confusion I noticed the turquoise blue silk scarf around the neck of the body inside the car. It had been a birthday present from a friend, someone I loved, and who I knew loved me, even thought that love was never enough to heal the pain inside or to still the cries of despair in my head. I scanned the rest of the body, moving closer, and item by item identified my jacket, my jeans, my ring. We don't usually see ourselves from outside our bodies, as others see us, and I felt disgusted at the sight of the pallid skin and lank, mousy brown hair, the worn hands still gripping the steering wheel with whitened knuckles and chewed finger nails. How could anyone ever love someone who looked like that? I deserved to die. But if that was 'me', who was 'I'? I certainly wasn't dead. I could see and feel my body. I could move, think, see, hear, smell. If I had somehow left the body in the car I certainly didn't want to go back to it; but how was I to die? Where was the dark nothingness I so craved?

The sound of a dog barking attracted my attention. A black Labrador belonging to our neighbor approached the car, hackles raised, giving a series of short staccato barks. His owner whistled from the next field but the dog edged closer to the car, barking more urgently. I tried to touch the dog, to hush it. We had always been friends, but this time the dog just barked even more loudly and insistently, the hair on the back of its neck and along its spine raised to give it a comical Mohican appearance. The owner approached, calling to the dog, who wasn't budging. I didn't want to be seen like that, or like this. I felt confused, shaken, and sort of drifted higher until I was looking down on the scene from directly above the car – a genuinely birds'-eye view. The man leant into the car, which I had evidently forgotten to lock, and turned the key in the ignition while holding a white handkerchief over his mouth and nose with his right hand. Once the engine had stopped running he backed off, pulling the dog, now on its lead, after him. I could see him get out his mobile phone and make a call, then stamp about a bit, looking impatiently at his watch.

Things started to happen quickly. It was like a detective programme on TV. A police car arrived, then an ambulance and then a second police car. It came down the misty lane with its siren whining, oddly muffled by the heavy morning air. It struck me as so incongruous in this quiet corner of the village, with pheasants strutting out of the hedges and across the wheat-ripening fields. They put yellow and black tape across the lane to block it off – not that many people come this way - and then a paramedic from the ambulance and a policeman tried to lift my body out of the car and onto a stretcher. It wasn't easy to prise the clawed hands from the wheel or extract the feet stuck under the pedals. I could see the effort it took; one had to go round the passenger side to lift the stiff, heavy legs while the other heaved the shoulders. I was suddenly glad that they didn't know me, embarrassed at all this fuss. I never liked drawing attention to myself. Then I followed the ambulance, not knowing what else to do, or where to go, assuming that when they resuscitated me I would find myself back in that body and my rotten, miserable, failed life. I wondered whether to run away so that I couldn't go back, but I wasn't dead yet and in this strange state didn't know how to finish the job I had started.

The next few days I hung around the morgue and even watched them bury me, although I didn't go into the church. I didn't want to speak to anyone, or make contact, either with the handful of mourners who seemed, somewhat to my surprise, to be genuinely grieving, or with the shady presences that never seemed to leave me quite alone, but who didn't show themselves fully either. Mostly I revisited places I had been, never straying too far from the physical body in the churchyard. I was aware of wispy white wraiths around some of the graves, like the smoke circles my uncle used to blow from his pipe, which held their form for a few seconds before dissolving into the air. I found some peace and solace sitting in my old haunt by the river – a large, flat boulder near a tangled sycamore that grew perilously near the bank. Its lower branches trapped the debris washed down by storms, providing a floating platform for coots and moorhens. A heron had its territory on the opposite bank, and would perch in a nearby tree when disturbed by canoeists or fishermen. It was as if I was waiting, but for what I couldn't say. I wasn't exactly miserable but it was as if my mind was stretching to remember something that kept slipping from my grasp, always just out of reach. I realized time had passed when the trees by the river and in the high wood where the badgers live began to turn, first some dusty yellows, followed by more vibrant russet reds, and eventually the copper brown of the great beeches. Then a fierce storm, the first of autumn, blew most of the leaves into the river and across the fields, leaving the trees bare and exposed to night frosts. The strange thing was that I no longer felt the cold, and needed no food or sleep. So days and nights passed in a kind of half-existence in which I was neither fully alive nor definitively dead.

Then Christmas arrived. I hated Christmas with a passion. I always felt so alone, so shamefully different. The jollity of other people, which often seemed forced and hollow, and the tackiness of the shops with their twinkling decorations and plastic Santas, drew up mingled despair and contempt in me. I wanted to run, to hide, to die. Usually I took a bottle of vodka to bed and tried to blot out the dreary, interminable days, hidden under my duvet in my miserable cold room that passed for home. Yet this time, despite myself, I found that I was being drawn towards the church. The bells were summoning people from the pubs and lighted homes to midnight mass. I drifted through the thick stone walls and into the warmth and light of the nave. As I hung there I became aware of a bright light, like a funnel, twisting down from the roof toward the altar. I hadn't been a regular church-goer since I was a child, but something about the smell of incense and the atmosphere within those walls lit a small flame of hope within me.

Some of the shadowy presences began to solidify, and mingling with the congregation in the pews, I saw my grandparents with my beloved old collie, a distant great aunt and other figures I didn't recognize, but all of whom were smiling kindly at me. As I took in the scene, the loving faces and outstretched arms, I suddenly knew that everything would be all right. 'It's time to go now,' my grandmother said, as she stepped forward and took my hand. I put my other hand on the dog's warm, silky head, and he reached up to nuzzle it with his soft, wet nose. Instead of the old stiff, blind dog who had been put to sleep more than a decade ago he was in his prime, as fit and lively as a three year-old. Together we walked toward the funnel of light, and as we were pulled effortlessly upwards, and out through the roof of the church, my surroundings faded. I knew that at last I was going home.

Wickland: *Can you tell us who you are?*

Spirit: *I can't seem to remember anything. What is the matter with my head? It is difficult for me to think. What kind of doctor are you?*

Wickland: *Medical. What is your name?*

Spirit: *My name? Strange I can't remember my name.*

Wickland: *How long have you been dead?*

Spirit: *Dead? I'm not dead. I wish I were.*

Wickland: *Is life so unpleasant?*

Spirit: *Yes it is. If I am dead then it is very hard to be dead. I have tried and tried to die... Why is it I cannot die?*

Wickland: *There is no actual death.*

Spirit: *Of course there is.*

Wickland: *How do you know?*[46]

...one cannot sufficiently stress the importance of directed prayer from friends or healing groups on earth in cases of suicide. They need the strength of our physical 'vibes' because of their own low vibratory state. It may even be easier for us on earth to contact them than for discarnate rescuers...

Now poor old D.J. Yes, I love him as we all do, and he is getting on; but he still can't forgive himself for failing to carry out the mission he undertook; it's a very common feeling among those who opt out, but it leaves a scar, and it has slowed up his development.[47]

[The etheric body] sometimes appears to those with whom it is closely bound up, as a cloudy figure, very dully conscious and speechless – the wraith. It may also be seen after the conscious entity has deserted it, floating over the grave where its dense counterpart is buried, slowly disintegrating as time goes on.[48]

When I work with clients who have committed suicide in former lives, the first thing most exclaim right after the moment of death is, 'Oh, my God, how could I have been so stupid!' These are physically healthy people, not those suffering from a debilitating physical illness. Suicide by a person, young or old, whose physical state has reduced the quality of their life to almost nothing is treated differently in the spirit world to those who had healthy bodies. While all suicide cases are treated with kindness and understanding, people who killed themselves with a healthy body do have a reckoning...

What happens to souls involved with suicide in healthy bodies? These souls tell me they feel somewhat diminished in the eyes of their guides and group peers because they broke their covenant in a former life. There is a loss of pride from a wasted opportunity. Life is a gift and a great deal of thought has gone into allocating certain bodies for our use. We are the custodians of this body and that carries a sacred trust...

In suicide cases involving healthy bodies, one of two things generally happens to these souls. If they are not a repeat offender, the soul is frequently sent back to a new life rather quickly, at their own request, to make up for lost time. This could be within five years of their death on Earth. The average soul is convinced it is important to get right back on the diving board after having taken a belly flop in a prior life. After all, we have natural survival instincts as human beings and most spirits tenaciously fight to stay alive.

For those who display a pattern of bailing out when things get rough there are places of repentance for a good purpose. These places do not contain a pantheon of horrors in some dark, lower spirit region reserved for sinners. Rather than being punished in some sort of bleak purgatory, these souls may volunteer to go to a beautiful planetary world with water, trees and mountains but no other life. They have no contact with other souls in these places of seclusion except for sporadic visits by a guide to assist them in their reflections and self-evaluation...Apparently this medicine seems to work because these souls come back to their groups feeling refreshed but knowing they have missed out on a lot of action and opportunities for personal development with their friends. Nonetheless, there are souls who will never adjust to Earth. I hear some are reassigned to other worlds for their future incarnations.[49]

We specially train thousands of spiritual beings who work tirelessly and constantly, helping and persuading people to be rescued, and also aid Rescue Circles on Earth who have experienced mediums that try to communicate with those lost souls. Controlled by Spirit, these specialised groups help those living in darkness to see the light, or persuade a waiting loved one to journey forward. It is at this point that they have to decide it is time for them to move away from the earthly ties and start their life in Spirit.[50]

In the world into which those freed from the physical body have gone, a loving thought is as palpable to the senses as is here a loving word or tender caress. Everyone who passes over should, therefore, be followed by thoughts of love and peace, by aspirations for his swift passage onwards through the valley of death to the bright land beyond.[51]

10. Time to Go

It is time to go, too late for second thoughts or hesitation. We have made our plans, rehearsed the details, laid trails, discussed our tactics and choices. No turning back now. And here I am, hurtling rapidly through space, getting faster, denser, smaller. I am attracting particles of increasingly heavy matter like iron filings to a magnet, astral matter that had once seemed as light and airy as a magic carpet now entangles me. Doubts are already creeping in – how will we recognize one another and what if one of us fails? The jaunty black hat, the cheap pizza restaurant. You are wearing green shoes. You will be twenty three, I am twenty five. It's your birthday party – I am carrying a bouquet of flowers for a girlfriend who doesn't show up. So many 'ifs'. What if...? What if my girlfriend forgets her part and comes along? Would it make a difference? If I'm not alone but walk in with someone else will our eyes still meet across the crowded room? My impatience might get the better of me again. I could be married with two kids, a cat and a budgerigar, and a mortgage by the time I'm twenty five. My wife might insist on cooking dinner at home that day to eat in front of the TV with the kids. And if we did meet and I was married, would that be better or worse? We have planned it to be a first love, a partnership for life. We will raise our children, sail round the world, have adventures and then grow old together. The darkness thickens and with a jolt I feel as if I have been squeezed through a narrow tube of toothpaste to land with a bump. A tiny heart beat, warmth. The gentle swaying motion of a country walk. Muffled voices. My consciousness shifts outside the tiny body to take a look at my new parents – it seems but a moment since we all rehearsed our roles, but in this heavy world of time they are already middle-aged, and looking forward to having this long-awaited first child. They look fit, happy, well-prepared, and the baby seems healthy. They have played their parts well. So far so good. Now I just need to remember the script, to play my part. No stage fright this time. I must give it my all.

To every Thinker, however unprogressed, there comes a moment of clear vision when the time arrives for his return to the life of the lower worlds. For a moment he sees his past and the causes working from it into the future, and the general map of his next incarnation is also unrolled before him. Then the clouds of lower matter surge round him and obscure his vision, and the cycle of another incarnation begins with the awakenings of the powers of the lower mind, and their drawing round them, by their vibrations, materials from the lower mental plane to form the new mental body for the opening chapter of his life-history.[52]

While some spiritual locales are difficult for my subjects to describe, most love to talk about the place of life selection, and they use remarkably similar descriptions. I am told it resembles a movie theatre which allows souls to see themselves in the future, playing different roles in various settings. Before leaving, souls will have selected one scenario for themselves. Imagine being given a dress rehearsal before an actual performance of a new life.[53]

...many soulmates have a preparation class just before their next incarnation. ... One aspect of this prep class might also include two soulmates going off alone and sending visual images to each other of what they will look like in their new human bodies and under what circumstances they are going to meet.[54]

Without knowing why, most people believe their life has a plan. Of course, they are right. Although amnesia does prevent having full conscious knowledge of this plan, the unconscious mind holds the key to spiritual memories of a general blueprint of each life.[55]

A...soul-self may be quite different or rather similar to the emotional temperament of their host body. Souls rely on spirit-world planners to find the best candidates for a partnership that will address their strengths and weaknesses. The choice of a particular body is intended to combine a soul's character defects and strengths with certain strong and weak emotional temperaments to produce specific trait combinations for mutual benefit. The biological mind of a human being is linked to a soul who then provides imagination, intuition, insight, and conscience. With this union we are one person dealing with two internal ego forces inside us during life. This combination represents the duality of mind and spirit in our bodies.[56]

The soul memory will go into the whole energy field of the baby...The human body is just an expression of what is in the energy field of the soul...When a soul chooses its form of incarnation, that choice covers everything: their parents, and how their DNA interacts to become the DNA of the fetus...It's an amazing synchronization of many energetic factors...This takes place before conception, it's in place from the moment the thought of that incarnation comes into being, it only takes a fraction of a second. But it would take infinity to truly understand in a scientific way, or to explain piece by piece, point by point.[57]

How important it is to learn to give ourselves absolutely![58]

Notes

1. C.W. Leadbeater (1912) *A Textbook of Theosophy.* Dodo Press, (pp.40 &55).
2. Hewitt, Susan (ed.) (2009) *The Eternal Truth: Spiritual teachings from Paul of Tarsus after two thousand years through the unique trance mediumship of Raymond Brown.* Scarborough: Tarsusco Ltd, (p.29).
3. Cynthia Sandys (1986) *The Awakening Letters: Volume Two.* Edited by Rosamond Lehmann. Saffron Waldon, Essex: C.W. Daniel, (p.42). Letter from Cynthia Sandys' brother Sir Alvary Gascoigne, known as Joe.
4. Cynthia Sandys and Rosamond Lehmann (1978) *The Awakening Letters: Varieties of Spiritual Experiences in the Life after Death.* Jersey: Neville Spearman, (p.27).
5. Cynthia Sandys and Rosamond Lehmann (1978) *The Awakening Letters: Varieties of Spiritual Experiences in the Life after Death.* Jersey: Neville Spearman, (p.48).
6. Cynthia Sandys and Rosamond Lehmann (1978) *The Awakening Letters: Varieties of Spiritual Experiences in the*

Life after Death. Jersey: Neville Spearman, (p.83). Communication from Father Andrew Glazewski.

7. Cynthia Sandys, *The Awakening Letters* Vol.2, (p.2).

8. Annie Besant & C.W. Leadbeater (1925) *Thought Forms.* Adyar: Theosophical Publishing House/Quest Books, (pp.72,76).

9. Cynthia Sandys, *The Awakening Letters,* (pp.101-2). Cynthia's mother to her brother Joe (both discarnate).

10. *Awakening Letters* Vol.2, (p.79). Edith Wood known as Edie.

11. Bill & Judy Guggenheim (1997) *Hello From Heaven.* New York: Bantam Books. Betty, 53 year old homemaker from Florida, (p.29).

12. Michael Newton, *Journey of Souls,* (p.27).

13. Michael Newton, *Journey of Souls,* (p.69).

14. Robert Schwartz (2009) *Your Soul's Plan: Discovering the Real Meaning of the Life You Planned Before You Were Born.* Berkeley, California: Frog Books, (p.206).

15. Cynthia Sandys, *The Awakening Letters,* (pp.130-131).

16. Michael Newton, *Journey of Souls,* (p.59).

17. Cynthia Sandys, *The Awakening Letters,* (p.13). Patricia's first letter.

18. Michael Newton, *Destiny of Souls,* (p.135).

19. Michael Newton, *Destiny of Souls,* (p.90).

20. C.W. Leadbeater, *A Textbook of Theosophy,* (p.51).

21. Cynthia Sandys, *The Awakening Letters,* (p.123). Patricia on her aunt Dorothy.

22. Hewitt, Susan (ed.) (2009) *The Eternal Truth: Spiritual teachings from Paul of Tarsus after two thousand years through the unique trance mediumship of Raymond Brown.*

Scarborough: Tarsusco ltd., (pp.30, 40-41).

23. C.W. Leadbeater (2006) *Astral Plane: Its Scenery, Inhabitants and Phenomena.* Filiquarian Publishing, (pp.50-51).

24. Cynthia Sandys, *The Awakening Letters*, (p.51). Letter from Joe, Cynthia's brother Sir Alvary Gascoine. 'Flo' is Florence Nightingale, Cynthia Sandys' first cousin twice removed, who continues her healing work on the 'other side'.

25. Annie Besant, *The Ancient Wisdom*, (p.61).

26. Cynthia Sandys, *The Awakening Letters*, Vol.2, (pp.70-71).

27. Cynthia Sandys, *The Awakening Letters*, Vol.2, (pp.24-5). Letter from Arthur, Cynthia Sandys' husband, Arthur Fitzgerald Sandys Hill, 6th Lord Sandys, Baron of Ombersley.

28. Hewitt, Susan, *The Eternal Truth,* (p.29).

29. Susan Hewitt, *The Eternal Truth*, (pp.28-9).

30. Susan Hewitt, *The Eternal Truth*, (p.59).

31. Cynthia Sandys, *The Awakening Letters*, (pp.18-19).

32. Annie Besant and C.W. Leadbeater (1925) *Thought-Forms*, (p.76).

33. Michael Newton, *Destiny of Souls*, (pp.210-12).

34. Cynthia Sandys, *The Awakening Letters*, Vol.2, (p.93). Letter from Edith Wood (Edie).

35. Ester and Jerry Hicks/The Teachings of Abraham (2008) *The Law of Attraction: How to Make it Work for You.* London: Hay House, (pp.65-6).

36. Chiara Lubich (2007) *Essential Writings*, New City: London, (pp.84-5).

37. Cynthia Sandys, *The Awakening Letters* Vol.2, (p.56).

38. Susan Hewitt (ed.), *The Eternal Truth*, (p.53).
39. Michael Newton, *Destiny of Souls*, (p.263).
40. Cynthia Sandys & Rosamond Lehmann, *Letters from our Daughters. Part 2: Patricia.* C.P.S. Paper No.2 (no date). London, (p.5).
41. Cynthia Sandys, *The Awakening Letters, Vol.2*, (p.85).
42. Annie Besant, *The Ancient Wisdom*, (p.83).
43. Robert Brain (1970) 'Friends and Twins in Bangwa' in Mary Douglas (ed.) *Man in Africa*. London, Tavistock, (pp.215-227).
http://www.lebialem.info/Brain1/braintwin.htm
44. Valerie Mason-John (2008) *The Banana Kid* London: BAAF, (pp.214-5).
45. Hewitt, Susan, *The Eternal Truth*, (p.52).
46. David Fontana (2009) *Life Beyond Death: What Should We Expect?* London: Watkins Publishing, (pp.72-3).
47. Cynthia Sandys, *The Awakening Letters* Vol.2, (p.13). Sally, Rosamond Lehmann's daugher.
48. Annie Besant, *The Ancient Wisdom*, (p.61).
49. Michael Newton, *Destiny of Souls*, (pp.153-6).
50. Susan Hewitt, *The Eternal Truth*, (p.29).
51. Annie Besant (1979) *Thought Power: Its control and culture.* Wheaton, Illinois: Quest Books/Theosophical Publishing House, (pp.109-110).
52. Annie Bessant, *The Ancient Wisdom*, (p.163).
53. Michael Newton, *Journey of Souls*, (p.207).
54. Michael Newton, *Destiny of Souls*, (p.274).
55. Michael Newton, *Destiny of Souls*, (p.213).
56. Michael Newton (2007) *Life Between Lives: Hypnotherapy for Spiritual Regression.* Woodbury, Minnesota: Llewellyn

Publications, (pp.183-4).

57. Ian Lawton (2007) *The Wisdom of the Soul: Profound insights from the life between lives.* Southend-on-Sea: Rational Spirituality Press, (p.42).

58. Cynthia Sandys, *The Awakening Letters*, Vol.2, (p.94). Letter from Edith Woods.

Bibliography

Besant, Annie (1977) [1897] *The Ancient Wisdom*. Adyar, Madras: Vasanta Press.

Besant, Annie (1979) *Thought Power: Its control and culture*. Wheaton, Illinois: Quest Books/Theosophical Publishing House.

Besant, Annie and Leadbeater, C.W. (1980) [1925] *Thought Forms*. Theosophical Publishing House, Adyar, Quest Books.

Brain, Robert (1970) 'Friends and Twins in Bangwa' in Mary Douglas (ed.) *Man in Africa*. London: Tavistock, (pp.215-227).
http://www.lebialem.info/Brain1/braintwin.htm

Fontana, David (2009) *Life Beyond Death: What Should We Expect?* London: Watkins Publishing.

Guggenheim, Bill and Guggenheim, Judy (1997) *Hello From Heaven*. Bantam Books: New York.

Hewitt, Susan (ed.) (2009) *The Eternal Truth: Spiritual teachings from Paul of Tarsus after two thousand years through the unique trance mediumship of Raymond Brown.*

Scarborough: Tarsusco Ltd.

Hicks, Ester and Hicks, Jerry /The Teachings of Abraham (2008) *The Law of Attraction: How to Make it Work for You*, London: Hay House.

Lawton, Ian (2007) *The Wisdom of the Soul: Profound insights from the life between lives*. Southend-on-Sea: Rational Spirituality Press.

Leadbeater, C.W. (1912) *A Textbook of Theosophy*. Dodo Press.

Leadbeater, C.W. (2006) *Astral Plane: Its Scenery, Inhabitants and Phenomena*. Filiquarian Publishing.

Lubich, Chiara (2007) *Essential Writings*, New City: London.

Mason-John, Valerie (2008) *The Banana Kid*. London: BAAF.

Newton, Michael (1995) *Journey of Souls: Case Studies of Life Between Lives*. Woodbury, Minnesota: Llewellyn Publications.

Newton, Michael (2007) *Life Between Lives: Hypnotherapy for Spiritual Regression*. Woodbury, Minnesota: Llewellyn Publications.

Newton, Michael (2008) *Destiny of Souls: New Case Studies of Life Between Lives*. Woodbury, Minnesota: Llewellyn Publications.

Sandys, Cynthia and Rosamond Lehmann (1978) *The Awakening Letters: Varieties of Spiritual Experiences in the Life after Death*. Jersey: Neville Spearman.

Sandys, Cynthia, selected and edited by Rosamond Lehmann (1986) *The Awakening Letters: Volume Two*. Saffron Waldon, Essex: C.W. Daniel.

Schwartz, Robert (2009) *Your Soul's Plan: Discovering the Real Meaning of the Life You Planned Before You Were Born*. Berkeley, California: Frog Books.

A Note on Sources

These short sketches are works of imagination, drawing upon my own everyday experience and that of people known to me, as well as many published sources. Examples from some of these sources are reproduced in italics, forming the second part of each chapter. The longer quotations form short stories in their own right. The information in these quotations comes by and large from four types of source material It is striking that despite their different origins, styles, emphases and details, a consistent picture emerges of life beyond the grave.

(1) Channelled material (acquired through mediumship and clairvoyance). A good example of material derived from mediumship are the letters received by Lady Cynthia Sandys. Lady Sandys discovered that she had the ability, while in a light trance, to receive communications from people in spirit, which she took down in the form of written letters. Most, although not all, of her interlocutors are immediate members of her family or former friends (her

father, husband, brother and daughter Patricia, for instance). This gives many of the *Awakening Letters* an intimacy and freshness that enables the reader to share the sense of discovery and wonder of Cynthia Sandys' discarnate inter-locutors as they explore life 'on the other side'.

(2) Material recorded from individuals undergoing past-life and interlife hypnotic regression. These accounts are usually published in the form of question and answer sessions between the therapist and client, together with additional commentary from the author/therapist. The quotations from Michael Newton and Andy Tomlinson fall into this category.

(3) Academic commentaries, usually drawing on both of the above sources, on near death experiences (NDE's), religious traditions, and insights from philosophy, science or literature, as in the work of David Fontana (among others).

(4) The Theosophical writings of Annie Besant (1847-1933) and C.W. Leadbeater (1847-1934) which, in many ways, anticipate more recent discoveries. Theosophy draws upon the esoteric traditions of many world religions (particularly Hinduism and Tibetan Buddhism). Besant and Leadbeater were heavily indebted to the writings and teachings of the founders of modern Theosophy, especially H.P. Blavatsky (1831-1891), as well as drawing upon their own 'occult' spiritual and clairvoyant experiences.

In addition to these varied but consistent sources of infor-mation I have drawn upon ethnography, fiction and spiritual writings. The message that shines through is that to live and die with an awareness of our identity as an eternal spirit eases our passage through the gate of death, and can inspire us to make the best possible use of our time on earth.

Acknowledgements

I would like to thank the following for permission to reproduce extracts from their published works:

The Awakening Letters: Varieties of Spiritual Experiences in the Life after Death and *The Awakening Letters: Volume Two* by Cynthia Sandys, edited by Rosamond Lehmann, reprinted by kind permission of the Random House Group and The Hon. Mrs Meriel Wingfield.

The Eternal Truth: Spiritual Teachings from Paul of Tarsus after two thousand years through the unique trance mediumship of Raymond Brown. Edited by Revd. Susan Hewitt. © Raymond and Gillian Brown, Susan Hewitt, Tarsusco Ltd. All rights reserved, used by kind permission of the publishers. Copies of this book are available from: www.raybrownhealing.com.

Destiny of Souls: New Case Studies of Life Between Lives by Michael Newton, PhD. © 2000 Llewellyn Worldwide, Ltd. 2143 Wooddale Drive, Woodbury, MN 55125-2989. All rights reserved, used by permission and with the best wishes of the publisher.

BOOKS

O is a symbol of the world, of oneness and unity. In different cultures it also means the "eye," symbolizing knowledge and insight. We aim to publish books that are accessible, constructive and that challenge accepted opinion, both that of academia and the "moral majority."

Our books are available in all good English language bookstores worldwide. If you don't see the book on the shelves ask the bookstore to order it for you, quoting the ISBN number and title. Alternatively you can order online (all major online retail sites carry our titles) or contact the distributor in the relevant country, listed on the copyright page.

See our website www.o-books.net for a full list of over 500 titles, growing by 100 a year.

And tune in to myspiritradio.com for our book review radio show, hosted by June-Elleni Laine, where you can listen to the authors discussing their books.

MySpiritRadio